Bears

Donna Bailey and Christine Butterworth

STECK-VAUGHN
LIBRARY
A Division of Steck-Vaughn Company

It is early morning on a hot summer's day.
This mother bear and her cubs
just woke up.
They are hungry after their night's sleep.

2

They are called grizzly bears because
their shaggy brown fur has white tips.
Grizzly bears live in North America.
They are very fierce and dangerous.

Bears like to live by themselves.
After mating, the male leaves the
female bear.
The mother grizzly lives with her cubs
in a den in the forest.

The cubs were born in the winter.
This cub is now three months old.
Its fur is still short and soft.

Now the cubs are six months old.
They like to play together and
pretend to fight each other.

The cubs follow their mother as
she digs in the ground for
roots to eat.
She shows them where to look for food.

The mother grizzly sees
a wild bees' nest hanging from
a branch above her head.
She hits it with her paw.
Bees buzz around her head and
try to sting her.

The grizzly yelps as a bee
stings her on the nose, but
she does not give up.
The nest falls to the ground
and breaks.
The bears lick out all the honey.
They think it is delicious!

9

Bears cannot see or hear very well, but
they have a very good sense of smell.
The cubs sniff at the earth.
They can smell the insects under the grass.
Bears eat insects, too.

The mother grizzly is still hungry.
She takes her cubs down to the river.

There are lots of other grizzlies there.
They have all come to catch
the salmon in the river.

The mother bear wades into the water.
Her cubs follow her.
She teaches her cubs how to catch
the salmon in the river.

The mother grizzly scoops the fish
out of the water with her paw.
She flips it onto a rock where
she can eat it.

Another grizzly wants to take away
her fish.
She snarls at the other bear and
bites him.
She sends the other bear away.

In the winter, snow covers the ground.
It is very cold, and the grizzly
can't find any food in the deep snow.
The grizzly and her cubs curl up
in their den and go to sleep.
They are hibernating.

16

All bears sleep a lot in the winter.
They only come out and walk around
if the days are sunny and mild.
This polar bear has come out of its den
to enjoy the sun.
Soon it will go back to its den to keep warm.

Polar bears live in the far north
in the cold Arctic.
The winter there is very long and dark.
The sea freezes, and snow
covers the land.

The polar bears make dens in the snow.
They stay in their dens until spring.

The mother bear and her cubs
huddle together to keep warm.
The cubs were born in the winter.

The mother bear feeds the cubs
with her milk.
She will teach them how to hunt for
seals and fish when they are bigger.

The cubs like to play on the ice.
They roll over and pretend
to bite each other.

Polar bears have huge paws with
long heavy claws.
The fur between their toes stops them
from sliding on the ice when they walk.

Polar bears can swim for miles
in the icy sea.
The mother bear dives under the water
to catch some fish.

24

Now the mother bear is tired.
She climbs out onto the bank and
shakes her long fur to get rid of
the icy water.

This bear is smaller than a polar bear.
It is an American black bear.
It has sharp teeth and long claws.

The bear is fighting a mountain lion.
The lion has sharp teeth too, but
the black bear is stronger than the lion.
It bites the lion and sends it away.

Black bears climb trees to look for
fruit and insects to eat.
Their long claws help them
hold onto the tree.

28

Even a little black bear cub
can climb trees.
This cub is resting on a branch.
In the tree it is safe from the mountain lion.

Giant pandas can also climb trees.
A giant panda is a special kind of bear.
It has thick, woolly, white fur with
black legs and black patches
around its eyes.

Pandas live in the forests and
mountains of China.
Their favorite food is the bamboo
that grows in the forests.

There are very few pandas left
in the world.
People cut down the bamboo forests,
and the pandas had nothing to eat.
Now people are trying to save the pandas
from dying out.

Index

black bear 26, 27, 28, 29

claws 7, 10, 12

climbing 28, 29, 30

cubs 2, 4, 5, 6, 7, 10, 11, 13, 16, 20, 21, 22, 29

den 4, 16, 19

fighting 6, 15, 27

fishing 13, 14

food 7, 9, 10, 12, 14, 21, 24, 28, 31

fur 3, 5, 23, 25, 30

hibernating 16, 17

mating 4

pandas 30, 31, 32

paws 8, 14, 23

play 6, 22

polar bears 17, 18, 19, 20, 21, 22, 23, 24, 25

river 11, 12, 13

smell 10

swimming 24

teeth 26

Reading Consultant: Diana Bentley
Editorial Consultant: Donna Bailey
Supervising Editor: Kathleen Fitzgibbon

Illustrated by Paula Chasty
Picture research by Suzanne Williams
Designed by Richard Garratt Design

Photographs
Cover: ZEFA
Bruce Coleman: title page, 3, 28 and 29 (Erwin & Peggy Bauer), 5, 13, 14, 20
    and 22 (Leonard Lee Rue), 11 (Jeff Foott), 17 (W. W. F./Thor Larsen),
    21 (B. & C. Alexander), 25 (Norman Owen Tomalin), 26 and 27 (Jonathan
    Wright), 30 (W. W. F./Kojo Tanaka), 13 (W. W. E./Timm Rautert)
Frank Lane Picture Agency: 2, 6, 10, 16 and 24 (Mark Newman), 4 (Gosta Tysk),
    7 (C. Rhode), 12 (Leonard Lee Rue), 23 (C. Carvalho)
OSF Picture Library: 15 (Frank Huber)
ZEFA: 32

Library of Congress Cataloging-in-Publication Data: Bailey, Donna. Bears/Donna Bailey and Christine Butterworth.
p. cm.—(Animal world) SUMMARY: Discusses the characteristics of different kinds of bears and also introduces the panda.
ISBN 0-8114-2633-5 1. Bears—Juvenile literature. [1. Bears. 2. Giant panda.] I. Butterworth, Christine. II. Title. III. Series:
Animal world (Austin, Tex.) QL737.C27B344 1990 599.74'446—dc20 89-22015 CIP AC

2 3 4 5 6 7 8 9 LB 96 95 94 93 92 91 90